STARS PRINCIPAL

STARS PRINCIPAL

POEMS BY

J. D. McCLATCHY

Macmillan Publishing Company · New York

Collier Macmillan Publishers · London

Macmillan Publishing Company
866 Third Avenue, New York, N.Y. 10022
Collier Macmillan Canada, Inc.

Grateful acknowledgment is made to the editors of the following magazines where poems in this book first appeared: *The Antioch Review, Grand Street, Ironwood, The Nation, The New Republic, The New Yorker, The Paris Review, Pequod, Ploughshares, Poetry, Poetry Review* (London), *Shenandoah, 2PLUS2*.

Eight of the "North Country Sketches" first appeared in a limited folio edition entitled *Lantskip, Platan, Creatures Ramp'd*, illustrated by Billy Sullivan and published by Parenthèse Signatures.

Library of Congress Cataloging-in-Publication Data
McClatchy, J. D., 1945–
Stars principal.
I. Title.
PS3563.A26123S7   1986   811′.54   85-30933
ISBN 0-02-582960-2

10 9 8 7 6 5 4 3 2 1

Book design by Joe Marc Freedman
Printed in the United States of America

For my parents

But if a man would be alone,
let him look at the stars. The
rays that come from those heavenly
worlds will separate between
him and what he touches.

—Emerson

Les riches plafonds,
Les miroirs profonds,
La splendeur orientale,
Tout y parlerait
A l'âme en secret
Sa douce langue natale.

—Baudelaire

Contents

IV

Stars
Principal

At a Reading

Anthony Hecht's

And what if now I told you this, let's say,
By telephone. Would you imagine me
Talking to myself in an empty room,
Watching myself in the window talking,
My lips moving silently, birdlike,
On the glass, or because superimposed
On it, among the branches of the tree
Inside my head? As if what I had to say
To you were in these miniatures of the day,
When it is last night's shadow shadows
Have made bright.
                Between us at the reading—
You up by that child's coffin of a podium,
The new poem, your "Transparent Man," to try,
And my seat halfway back in the dimmed house—
That couple conspicuous in the front row
You must have thought the worst audience:
He talked all the while you read, she hung
On *his* every word, not one of yours.
The others, rapt fan or narcolept,
Paid their own kind of attention, but not
Those two, calm in disregard, themselves
A commentary running from the point.
Into putdown? you must have wondered,
Your poem turned into an example, the example
Held up, if not to scorn, to a glaring
Spot of misunderstanding, some parody
Of the original idea, its clear-obscure
Of passageways and the mirrory reaches
Of beatitude where the dead select
Their patience and love discloses itself
Once and for all.
              But you kept going.
I saw you never once look down at them,
As if by speaking through her you might
Save the girl for yourself and lead her back

To your poem, your words to lose herself in,
Who sat there as if at a bedside, watching,
In her shift of loud, clenched roses, her hands
Balled under her chin, a heart in her throat
And gone out in her gaze to the friend
Beside her. How clearly she stood out
Against everything going on in front of us.

It was then I realized that she was deaf
And the bearded boy, a line behind you,
Translating the poem for her into silence,
Helping it out of its disguise of words,
A story spilled expressionless from the lip
Of his mimed exaggerations, like last words
Unuttered but mouthed in the mind and formed
By what, through the closed eyelid's archway,
Has been newly seen, those words she saw
And seeing heard—or not heard but let sink in,
Into a darkness past anyone's telling,
There between us.
                        What she next said,
The bald childless woman in your fable,
She said, head turned, out the window
Of her hospital room to trees across the way,
The leaflorn beech and the sycamores
That stood like enlargements of the vascular
System of the brain, minds meditating on
The hill, the weather, the storm of leukemia
In the woman's bloodstream, the whole lot
Of it "a riddle beyond the eye's solution,"
These systems, anarchies, ends not our own.

The girl had turned her back to you by then,
Her eyes intent on the thickness of particulars,
The wintery emphasis of that woman's dying,
Like facing a glass-bright, amplified stage,
Too painful not to follow back to a source
In the self. And like the girl, I found myself
Looking at the boy, your voice suddenly

Thrown into him, as he echoed the woman's
Final rendering, a voice that drove upward
Onto the lampblack twigs just beyond her view
To look back on her body there, on its page
Of monologue. The words, as they came—
Came from you, from the woman, from the voice
In the trees—were his then, the poem come
From someone else's lips, as it can.

I

Change of Scene

Where Love's a grown-up God

1. The Cup

The figures on this morning's second cup
Slowly wake to a touch whose method
Varies. My finger's circling outside the fire-
Charged sunrise saucer and the cloud
Chip on its rim, while the sugary anthem
Of dregs inside, struck up to call a halt

To dreaming, turns strangely bitter. Halting,
Blind, it's they who finger the lip of the cup.
Hoplite or sharecropper, can I speak for them?
A grown-up love asks a relentless method.
They swarm like ghosts to the bloody cloud
Of thought: what of my life, where's my fire?

One of them bends now to spit in the fire.
The only hesitation is of flame, its halt
Or stutter, as when the heart bolts out of a cloud
Long enough to light what's fallen to the cup's
Dark side to show, illustration's methodical
Storm of types. Two chances. Which of them

Is mine? The horse and rider's winded anthem?
Or the thumbprint ash, arms akimbo, blackfired
Against the light? Oh, love's our method
To let blood put on the skyspan halter,
That bit of thinking, then ride, then cup
The dawn in a cold hand. The cloud

Parts again. Moon mouth half shut on cloud.
Star crumbs. A woman rising to leave them
To themselves. She's overturned their cup
Of responsibilities, spilling it into the fire's
Airglow. And when she asked whose fault
It was, I had to choose between old methods

Of excess. You'll hear I chose that myth odd
To some, even to her, and know how it would cloud
Any fear of hers to make time pass or halt
On that one moment. The myth holds one of them—
I mean now one of us—up to the fire
Already gone out from the body, as into a cup,

Its thirsts poured into another cup, a method
To balance the fire's given set of words, a cloud
That drifts over them before it halts at *sorrow*.

2. The Method

When you're away I sleep a lot,
Seem to pee more often, eat
Small meals (no salad), listen
To German symphonies and . . . listen.

Sympathy, more often than not,
Is self-pity refined to Fire
And German Symphonies. *Nun lesen.*
Read a book. Write "The Method."

Or is self-pity, refined, two fires
Seen as one? Instructions collapse:
Write the book. (Read: a method.)
The hearth's easy, embered expense,

Seen as one instruction, collapses
In the blue intensity of a match.
The heart's lazy: remembrance spent
Forgetting. Love, break a stick.

In the blue intensity of as much
It is bound to catch—the far away—
Forgetting love. Break a stick.
The flames are a reward, of sorts.

They're bound to reach that far away.
The book says so. And who can't say
The flames are his reward? Of course
They are dying. Still, they scorch

The book. Say so, and—two can play—
Fires kindle (*smack!*) their own display.
They are dying, still. How they scorched
When I put this light to time.

Kindled fires smack of their own display.
Of smaller denials, no saying. Listen:
Where I put this light, it's time,
When you're away, asleep, or lost.

3. Démesure

Once, at last, the knives thrown down,
In each glass's sinking heart
A forgotten acid drop of wine
Both tongues had tried to dwell on,
I reached across the table.
Would you dare refuse that art
So far gone into, so sadly able?

But simply grasped, a hand
Will pull back, if it can,
That holds what's bound to give:
Then give me what I have.

The fog in a voice on the radio lifts
As it tells the time. Midnight. Yet
We two stay on either side of sense,
Wandering Reason and his witness Regret.

4. The Forest Fire

In the stalls of fir and oakenshaw, a song
    So faint yet nearing it sounds to the ear
That listens now from my room, at a distance of years,
Of the first alarm, a wet ash on the tongue

That, swallowed, burst the throat of a wailing bear
    Who turned and bit and tore himself,
The flame like a dog on his back, or a consuming belief.
Blood ran black from his mouth, and ascended the air.

The sticky cloud swells, then disappears
    As suddenly as each tree—the ash
In the eye, nerves ramifying, its glass
Hermit crazed and hanging inside a tear.

All's inverted there, and nothing keeps
    Itself but blackened by reverse.
The sky looks so, the cloud-crossed house,
To a man just drowned. And to you perhaps.

I can hear you, running in a staggered circle,
    Shouting to save us all, straw
And bone, the dove in panic, the child who crawls
Into a beckoning light, the whitetail's skull

Already seized by fire-claws. The forest,
    Starved with delays, is the latest dreamer.
A racking thunder spasm wants to clamor
And rescue to find us in a drizzle of sparks

Thrown down with the wood, and soon scattered.
    There may still be an echo of that fire
In anyone's heartbeat. But what I hear
Is light tapping quick upon the shutter.

5. The Cloud

Then I went out into a body of voices,
And the voices rose, the body of a cloud,
The cloud carried by the weight of bodies
Pulling against the plectrum of that pine
Like chimney smoke over the frame house,
Dayfall's refrain and fingers of light
At the window, a boy with his cup full
Taken into the cloud. He'll serve,

Taken up as into a confidence. The cloud
Pauses to come by momentum from the common
Life, bends to its water now, consents
To chase the dead to earth, and, lightened
Of all but a loneliness, keeps the boy
To leave him in another place picked out
From memory. A sudden guest of the wind,
He enters as accident, all the day can speak.

6. *Anthem*

All things began in separation: the day's
Young god, puffed, fireshod, first dispatched
On a mirrored globe: the negress, locked up
In a star chamber, her lamp at the lone window:
Dry land parted from sea, its knobby fruit
Spilt from river urns, the spring's leaking
Pitcher drawn up from the airy stream: wave's
Spume breaks on a caudal fin, shells soften
To paws: then the clouds too will take shape
As stag and hen, infant owl who repeats—*who?*

Made of something missing, the couple comes:
His city in flames, a stitch in his side
From having run this far away from home,
He dreams his heart's a book, open to her
Taper's hovering wing: call him again:
He had not meant so much he could not see
The worst that love can do: to wake and leave
Loving, indifferent to practice this one way:
But who will believe me if I say he fell
Into some deeper sleep: in the end was a word.

7. *The Halt*

The bricks pale, two by two, behind the fire
Laid across dread-hot dragontails.
One ear cocked for a free lance, you're stalled
Above—or no, *below*—tonight's pyre
Of loveknots quite untied in style. Whose scales
Stake me? you ask. For that matter, inspire?

Or so you'd write, set straight, complain
To me of love, as I did once to you:
Another two-faced coinage of the brain
Torn between wishbone and lyre,
Old tuning fork, divining rod
Good for what it can least afford.

That loophole made by any pair of pain
Now bent toward, now away from the very word
To free them of its liberties, is where you
Stay, as in a tarnished oval locket—picture
It!—worn sometimes, against all odds
I might have taken, even thought to blame

Without you then. Which of us cared, you knew,
That black penpointed tears would be as vain
As mine were back when. The feelings, too.
It seems (the flames are sputtering) so long since
We set off under false colors like compliments,
The lovely parts that grieve and then grow true.

The Palace Dwarf

The Ladder of Paradise would lead, this time,
　　To the Apartment of the Dwarfs, the steps
　　　　So short the rise was gradual as an afterlife.
　　The French looked at pictures in their guidebooks
　　　　As it was described. The Germans whispered
Loudly to each other. I watched the dwarf

Climb the stairs. I had spotted him the day before,
　　Flat on a wall by the Mincio, reading *Emma*.
　　　　That was put aside, some scenes too clogged
　　With allusion, like the river with its frisbees,
　　　　Detergent jugs, weeds in cellophane barettes.
But here he was again. No gainsaying the insistent,

Good and evil alike. Which did he seem, in sunglasses,
　　A studded motorcycle jacket, smudge of sideburns,
　　　　Tattooed crown of thorns? His baby-head
　　Bulged with its one secret, how to turn anyone's
　　　　Gold back into straw, this whole palace—
Ticket-booth, fresco, tourist group, the long galleries

Overthrown with history—into a dropcloth, a slatting
　　Canvas yanked aside from plaster-frame ambition,
　　　　The heart made small with scorn of littleness.
　　Did he feel at home here, where only he could
　　　　Fit? But who ever does? Head bowed now
In self-defense, I followed him up the tilting

Scale, from the chapel, its breadbox altar and gnarled
　　Crucified savior, in death near lifesized for him,
　　　　Back to the bedrooms and the favorite's gilded
　　Manger. Not a word, not a wink. He took it all in,
　　　　Or all but what was missing, any window view
That gave out on "the former owner's" contradictions,

A garden's logic of originality, the box-hedged
       Bets, the raging winged cypresses, the royal
              Children playing with their head-on-a-stick,
       The jester's marotte, over whose cap they'd look
              Back, up at the Apartment, that skewed cortex
Through which I wormed behind him. How close

It had suddenly become, when as if into the daylight
       That jabs a shut eye from between the curtains
              Of his dream, we were led into the next room,
       Where guardian archers had once been posted,
              Their crossbows ready for the unseen nod,
Their forty horses stabled in paint above.

Each niche turned a knotted tail impatiently.
       Instinct looks up. But where one expected
              Allegory, the simple bearings that tell us
       Where and how tall we ought to stand—some titan
              Routing the pygmy appetites, some child
Humbling kings to their senses—the ceiling's frame

Of reference was empty—the missing window at last?—
       Clouds bearing nothing. And nothing was what
              We were certain of. We looked around
       For the dwarf, the moral of these events.
              He was waddling out of a far door, as if
He knew where next we all would want to be.

A Cold in Venice

Montaigne—for him the body of knowledge
Was his own, to be suffered or studied
Like a local custom—had one too, I read
In bed, his diary more alert and all-gathering
The more I lose touch with it, or everything.
Even the gardenia on the neighbor's sill
That for three nights running a nightingale
Has tended with streamsprung song—
The senses competing with a giddy vulgarity—
Draws a blank. The San Vio vesper bells
Close in, fade, close in, then fade
To the congestion of voices from the street.

Why "clear as a bell"? Even as the time-release
Capsule I'm waiting on is stuffed with pellets
The bell must first be choked with the changes
To be rung, all there at once, little explosions
Of feeling, the passages out of this world.

These pills clear a space, as if for assignment
Undercover. Last week's liver seared in oil
And sage, the mulberry gelato on the Zattere . . .
Neither smell nor taste make it back.
And what of the taste for time itself,
Its ravelled daybook and stiff nightcap,
What it clears from each revisited city,
Depths the same, no inch of surface unchanged?
I can see to that. The gouged pearl pattern
Of light on the canals, the grimy medallioned
Cavities of the facings, or goldleaf phlegm
Around a saint's head. It's always something
About the body. For Montaigne the cure
Was "Venetian turpentine"—grappa, no doubt—
Done up in a wafer on a silver spoon.
The next morning he noticed the smell
Of March violets in his urine.

                                    How dependent
One becomes on remedies, their effects familiar
As a flower's perfumed throat, or a bird's
Thrilled questioning, like the trace
Of a fingertip along that throat, or now
Between the lines of a book by someone well
I'd taken up to read myself asleep with.

Perseid Shower

At this angle to the rest of it—
The turtle's back now foam rubber,
And at such an incline drop after drop
Of triple sec dribbles through my beard,

As if to douse the Old Gold
Downstream on my lap—they make sense.
Relax. It's happening. Forgive them.
They know what they are doing.

Like that first dormitory shower,
Its grudging spit and stub of fire,
A damp towel-snap the halfback
Thought one worthy of. Desire

Takes its shapes. They still
Show the chains at Joppa where
Someone, stripped to her jewels,
Was held to a promise. The ex-wife

Beside me a sudden chill
Has made the watchful virgin.
"They fly in pairs, an atmosphere
Between them." *That* makes

For minutes we can talk over
The trouble of being saved,
You from him, me for her—
That coral reef a scare gave

The ocean face-down. Looking
Up at it, the small lives
In its grip, shall we agree
To love what's sent and gives?

Now the others show up, one
In white jigging over the lawn.
Who'll spot him? Who's free
To choose knows best. Not me.

Overdoing it as usual, afoot
With some brimming self-regard,
He's all our love in the dark
Out here, abandon that would

Set us right—there's
Another!—to what we'd missed.
So much closer than one cares
Is whom we long to kiss.

Three Conversations

with the sculptor Natalie Charkow

1.

Silence. The extremities. More private still
        the parts raw stone, untouched,
   an arm's length from that far coast of thigh
    and full-moon nipple. What are his hands
      into now? They prompt where they would
     calm *last time now.*

The sense accelerates. His guards, to steady
       himself, a candle flame,
   all the light we read by: her pale
    reflection on him, shivering
      as he asks, then withdraws a question,
     is what I see.

And if I could say "our" instead of "private"?
       But I am no more that
  figure than you are who made it,
    pinching the wick-lashed shadows lost
      in conversation. Nostalgia's what
     you insist on.

2.

The next decade's steep descent, back to those heights
       from which, made and given,
  all measure, the template of myth comes.
    Nine possibilities standing in
      for each other, and a god to choose.
     Something tugs. It's—

Longing? For what? Perhaps one muse's foresquare
       scene with Apollo. She's
 self- effacing, "a chronicle
   of her kind." And lackadaisical
      History has been pointing to
     wizened harpies

swooping into life. So little the others—
    whole notes crimped on one's reed,
another's fluted skirt a match for
    the column's—seem to care about us,
        it's true, then, what they say. Fiddle,
        pose, lunge backwards,

then up to the god. So much less *he* must feel
        of late, thick folds of Self
worn over the shoulder. Signs are
    posted everywhere. There—those head-sized
        skulls start a hammering on the heart
        under the stone.

3.

"Suppose"—suppose that were the subject, and based
        where, certain of herself
and of too little else, she would lie,
    body put aside for the idea
        of body. It leaps from her hands.
        She's closed her eyes:

Woman Turned into Herself, Cat Watching Her.
        Drumhead hollows inside
have their own designs, the slow exchange,
    pulse for claw that digs into the skin,
        one life for its own. Tonight wants
        its share. Again

in the dark, she hides her hands under her hair.
        It falls loosely across
    the gaze of a god. He won't stir,
        but waits to count on his other lives.
        No one has come yet to tell him
        another's due.

Wells River

We went along a way we'd gone before,
This time alone—up, against the lash
Of a stream bed where in spring, fools-thaw
Past, the cold year pours down out of itself
The way the will moves toward the term
It has elected, but then of course was dry,
Needled by fall to a dull gloss on itself
That lapped the fieldstone, the fern-locks.
I'd knelt to pick apart a cone of chrysalis.

I mention the details to remind you
Of the give-and-take. You were scuffing
At mossdown, pointing to changes swollen
With growth and decay but no quickening choice,
And to a pair of braided, fluent birches.
"Why aren't *we* alone more often?" Words
That, when I look up too quickly still,
Make me see double to where you stood.
I mean I am *here*, and at the same time *then*,
Your hand as suddenly in mine as I'd reached up,
And the sense of a life together that sounds
A counterforce of wavering,
That change of mind this incline of months
Sends back and forth and back again.

And, as today I woke in the hammock,
Late sunlight daydreaming beside me,
My arm dangling over the side, elbow-deep,
It seemed the way before us had become
A kind of inlet, a needle-eye inlet
On the river, us both a boy in his skiff,
With a basket of food, his retriever.
(What had I been dreaming of before?
What calm regrets, anticipations
Of more than was reflected in some deep
Or exaggerated swerve of light on my face?)
He was moored to a swayback willow.
If setting out, I could have reached down
To loosen the rope, as any friend might
Who had (—I had) our walk in mind.

The Lesson in Prepositions

de

The night watchman, Mr. Day,
having let us in, the elevator's
pneumatic breath is held,
counting now again to ten.
It's we who wonder what's up.
Arriving there follows after
a loss—is it of that push-
button Panic, or Power's pulley?—
over any grounds for leaving.
The rule is, if you try to hurt
by silence, you'll find the words
to accuse yourself of speech.
Time to talk back. Say *here*, *out*.
The fingertipped light's gone out.

ex

Because the door automatically slid
closed against a pointless kiss—
an ashen sulphur-bulb still smoking—
and by reason of a walk refused
out of a mood since despaired of
for effects . . . no, wait for me!
If you'll apologize, I'll go.

sine

The way the dead live in dreams
as ageless ego's poor relation,
the milksop or wattled Muscovy duck,
every feature, under a merciful eye,
concentrated on "Did you *ever* love me?"
—so there you are, without an answer.

sub

My friend the screenwriter,
the moth in Armani fatigues
under cover of flickering credits,
is in from the coast and down

on his luck. "You've no idea
what it's like to loll
in the hold. The whisperjet
full of studio spies could talk
of nothing else." At the foot of having
been left to myself, I could
only think of our old days out back,
Vantages lit, the stock company
of headmasters left to the dishes.
We were playing the Landscape Game.
House. Key. Body of water. Beast.
A bowl stood in for art. Yours
had legs that ran all the way home.
It was a backdoor in summer,
your mother calling through
the half-patched screen. The fireflies
in your jar brightened when you shook.

ad

The new stars are coming out.
To ward off another influence
is one priority, but only one.
The other is to catch their light
as a design on us, then call it
hardship up among the heroes.
I go back to what falls
out as advance. Call their bluff
a cloud that blurs the dark
retreating densities. Or call it
hardship, then call to it again
and hear answer: *come up here*
and see for yourself. Even then
I went ahead and answered back.
Who has the last word wins
his forced smile, but only one.

cum

With what? The too familiar
self that ducks behind depressions,

a cigarette and shot on the landing?
The estranged hubbub of dressing?
How often can one ask, how
do I look? I look alone,
perched in this mare's nest
of cross-hatched fume and twig.
The newel-post could be a trunk
(packed with, oh, rings of age)
to climb back down on.
This once there's a footstep,
an echo, a step, then a step.

pro

As good as guilt in front
of his floor-length plea
for the short view of sincerity,
even the blackest has side.
When he's right, I'm left
donned in flawless arraignment.

post

What's over takes the accusative,
shears to the podded scape, shovel
down on the woodchuck's skull,
the humbling touch, or misfingered
bagatelle that bears down not on
but as the moment. The point's
to add dependence whether or not
you have the means to support it,
a pedal weight that sticks,
like blood, like brooding,
to make a fool of motive,
love's long held embarrassment.

After a Visit

"The surest way to the center is through a maze,"
The guide was saying. A thread snapped, so.
Its pain outlasts the calm receding daze.

Foreplay, partita, the faint slurred phrase
From the deathbed, each a lucid vertigo . . .
The surest way to the center is through a maze.

Itself the object of its search, the soul strays
Homeward, daunted by all it used to know.
Its pain casts out the calm receding daze.

Reason's monster—bull-headed, overpraised—
Lifts himself up from the blood in the throat.
The surest way to a center is through his maze.

Can you remember the spiralling scar I raised
Before you flinched, and not wanting to let go
Its pain? Out past the calm receding days

Since, I've learned to love in random ways
You predicted then, a long way back, though
The surest way to the center is still that maze
Where pain outlasts the calm receding daze.

II
North Country
Sketches

Fiddlehead

The inward turn of mind,
A hymn-bright coil closed
Down with its fervent clutch
Of six like-minded believers,

A backwoods congregation,
The ground broken like bread
Over histories of leafmat
Between light and death.

Each soul shreds its own.
What little, what lot is left
To clear the throat—dirt
Crystal, crackling parchment,

The dying rise of seasons—
Is coughed up. *Distraction's*
Beyond my moral, not Jack-
In-the-pulpit, not the trillium's

Scarlet letter. I've survived
Out here. Here's the counter-
Culture, beads of thaw-sweat,
Roots in acid, outstretching

Arms, a sharp-toothed pamphlet
Miniature of the point in each,
Less to read time after time
Until it's been made. It says,

[Something] Saves. Hard to make
Out, they're in such a hurry
To ascend. Not long it's a high
Church crozier, the flock around

Of hepatica in starched collars.
Beliefs change, harden.
Take that thin rib, the west
Drawn out of east, who would

Have thought how it turns out?
Not the sun on its frond of horizon,
A port-flushed vicar nodding
Off behind the potted fern.

Bees

First to bloom at last
    this late spring
the crabapple's a wain
    of white the ox
sun is hauling homeward.

Humbles brawl on top,
    goaded by syrups,
the rut of work so far
    from the wing-lit
hive of their making.

A bent toward folly argues
    for intelligence.
They'll break with the past
    as with an enemy.
The flowers cry to them!

          *   *   *

Left behind, in clover's
    common sense,
a solitary honeybee
    plies her trade.
Circumspect, all twelve

thousand eyes are trained
    on her needlework:
genetic cross-stitch
    and pollen purl.
Her pattern is the field's.

Dragonfly

Itinerant clarinet
A celesta comb tunes with wings:
Bayadere on the Moor's back,
Amusing a fuzzy crowd busy
In Admiralty Square.

Its flight? Oh, the baggy clown's,
Mooning by day, collapsing at night
In a tiny starpatched sky loft
Where successive dreams muster
Scimitars, a fanfare of palms . . .

Shrovetide masqueraders
In a mob of selves that others see—
Devil-and-Goat, Eye-on-Broomstick,
Goblin tableaux over dome and cross.
They cannot scare but kill the clown.

One more quiver in that arrow.
Out of its wits, it wobbles, still.
—It's then the ghost appears, high
Over the plot, and on its particulars.
On the membraned leaf.

On the loosestrife's whips.
On the air. On my lips.

Grasshopper

```
G
  G
    G
      GOLD Goldsmith's . . .
      Runner? No,
        All
          Summer a topflight
          Scholar of stalks, in
            Herringbone (spiffy!) plus-fours,
              Odd-lot jumper, clawed plimsolls, aviators—
              Parsing the leaflet's old tag:
              PERTINAX AUREUM
                ERRORQUE
                RERUM
                  R
                    R
                      R
                        R
                          R
                            R
```

Snake

Close by the creepered wall,
On the cinquefoil's shaggy border,
He takes the sun, and the unwary fly.
The snake is named Disorder.

This garter's all reversed,
Elastic frayed, the yellow stripe
Of species a dirty, bulging seam—
Precision's antitype.

He's a pile of himself!
Too old, too devil-may-care. And yet . . .
That staring eye and wrap-around grin
Unearth a buried debt.

To what? You back away,
Then turn to cultivate some quarter
Of the garden, sulking rows that say
The snake is named Disorder.

On a Blade of Grass

MATING SNAILS
shell's hachured demilune greige
bunchbacked shrug of mucilage in
horned question ark gravity's up
ended out of itself of out ended
up gravity's ark question horned
in mucilage shrug of bunchbacked
greige demilune's hachured shell
SNAILS MATING

Swift

I caught this evening
    evening's headliner,
        darkling-dusk-drawn

Dauphin of the air, riding
    high, chimney to riffs
        around the juniper.

Valance and tact, oh, dare,
    glide, and off on swing,
        japanned crossbow,

No buckle but on the toe—
    a syncopated third told
        lovelier—of wing,

Of plume, mastery of things
    with bite that—SLAP!—
        mill to improvise

By flits and starts: *Mayfly,*
    Mosquito, Gypsy Moth . . .
        the night club routine.

Hummingbird

There is no hum, of course, nor is the bird
That shiver of stained glass iridescence
Through which the garden appears—itself
In flight not from but toward an intensity
Of outline, color, scent, each flower
An imperium—as in a paragraph of Proust.

Mine is a shade of that branch it rests on
Between rounds: bark-wing, lichen-breast,
The butternut's furthest, hollow twig.
How to make from sow thistle to purslane?
So, into this airy vault of jewelweed,
Slipped past the drowsing bee watch,

Deep into the half-inch, bloodgold
Petal curve, tongue of the still untold.
Deaf to tones so low, the bees never mind
The dull grinding, these rusted gears
Pushed to the limit of extracting
From so many its little myth of rarity.

Dead Elm

House tree,
Sovereign heart-
Bound scan,

Overarmed
Terrorist of each
Shoot below and bud

That lean away
Toward a light
Daily more brilliant

Than before the rot
That took, whited
Crotch to tip.

Phosphorescent
Outsized leaf's the moon
Now as never before.

Oh, what can she
Show me, cold breath
On your crazed plate,

I could not have seen
Behind the papery
Ovate wings of will

—To die, it now seems.
That disease. Myth
And the slippery distance.

Spider

By this time of year asparagus matters
Less than my hill of beans about to wilt
Under the feathery nimbus of shade
Cast by select escapees from the table.
So I set a day to lash them with jute
Against the siren song of their decline
Into next year's growth, then cut back
The useless females, spindly, berry-bobbed
Sorts that would scatter their own kind
And weaken my stock of reasonable males.

One knotted to the paling, two down,
And the third frightens me out of my
Knack for distinguishing trope from type.
(A Field Guide later sets it to rest:
The Nursery Web.) She's made her bed,
All canopied with gauze, and laid in it
Her seasonal sac, burst into a pendant
Fleshpot . . . how many thousand young?
But where one might expect a swarming
Is the calm of form, a tent of Israel,

Magnified smear-slide of reflection
On itself. Watch it, all and each, gather
Its now thousand-fold strength to do
The same on every spear next spring.
Any chaos small enough to see—canticle
Of white cells run amok, or spinneret
Loops of Zen—undoes the impulse
To destroy it. Here, an eye's measure
Spilling out of itself, like meaning,
Helplessly, the phantom web of signs.

What's the matter? Talk of sibling
Rivalry? The pack of one's peers?
Leaf and limb here clinch on purpose.
She's out of bed now, up on three pairs
Of unshaved legs in hockey knee-socks:

Herself! gawky matrix of this song,
The shape these would-be lives fulfill,
Until I cut the stem. If I do.
What resists my shears is sheer
Conformity. Why not leave it to her,

Suspended on her belief in something more
And more the same, a sunlit protein force
Like constant fire crawling on a wick
Aflicker with the future? Where I would
Not kill, they'll kill a lower class
And serve them up as courtship gifts,
Weave winter tales between iris and aster
That tell me what I do not want to hear,
The old story of spending and begetting.
Why is it what's ugly tells the truth?

Tree Frog in a Rose

The unlikely once in place
There is no sensible echo,
No solid but rippling surface
In today's overblown ideal,
And no attendant delay
Of evolutionary scale.
What any cave of origin,
Or mirrored wall (stepping
Down its showcase the couple
Sees a dozen mornings stem)
Might expect, the serial glint
Of various distances, is dubbed
In by the old familiars—
"*Loved her, hated him*"—
The scratchy groove in the voice,
Stale perfume in the crease.

                    *   *   *

The night before the threatened revolution
They are at a ball—not one of the best—
And by this time outside, in the garden.
She has turned back, but into a moon cloud
That changes her. He stoops to free her gown
From the hawthorn hedge, and through it
Half glimpses the inconstant house, the music . . .

                    *   *   *

Of the spheres? Three rose petals
Of a nebula in the Archer's bow—shot!
Shot far beyond the starred scum of tree tops,

Your eye that seeds itself, like imperfection.

The blur in the spectrographer's foliate printout.

We know whose invisible worm, fat and smiling
In the fiery mab's unknowing embrace.

The Luna Moth

The calm after a storm brought out the stars.
Glowworms signalling up from the sopping grass, no matter
That shutters of rain had opened over them, were also stars
Reflected upon. But constellations abound—those stars
Cut in my old tin lantern that hangs these nights
By the back door, electrified with curiosity. The stars
It throws along the granite stoop are no less true stars
For being poor man-mades. Last night they drew nothing
At first. Then, a luna moth, who battered at nothing,
The window of a theme, each pane a star
Whose frame I'd opened on the fluorescence in the day-
Light tube over the stove left on for her. Come day,

The greasy copper colander that shines for us by day
Was no more moon but a sweet gum grove, the stars
Of her submarginal eyelet spots blind to the day
I'd stumbled down on. The problem: what to do today
With her, a washed-out beauty that lingers, like the Matter
Of Rome? The old chroniclers, in their day,
Knew that history was for "writing up." What each day
Dealt was blocked out on the wiped slate of that night's
Sky. Then the stories from Freud's couch set the mind's night-
Life on his ear, until those star-studded myths saw day
Again—as when at the Lido a horse conjured out of nothing
Plunges through spotlights into a tank of women wearing nothing

But spangled belts. I was fifteen. "Oh, it's nothing,"
My mother said, when I asked why she'd winced. "The day,
The whole day's been tiring." At that age, there is nothing
To disbelieve. Now I realize she was right. It *was* nothing,
A flying horse, four girls who wanted next year to be stars
Somewhere else. Even the program (my French was up to nothing
More) spoke of "*aspirations des artistes.*" There seemed nothing,
That first trip abroad, that didn't hum with "What's the matter?"
The hereditary instructions written down in every bit of matter
Might as well have read Mind and Eat It All and Touch Nothing,
Each nucleotide a stern look that *Might Have Consequences Tonight.*
And after that show, they did. No sooner in bed by midnight,

I had sneaked out of the hotel, determined only at night
Would any City of Light appear. I found next to nothing
From my Guide Noir. Cafés touted as *"les gares de la nuit"*
Were a wood of murmuring cognac leaves too soon ignited
By a deep inhale. The pissoir's perforated necessity (that day
I had slipped in one and been scolded) was, overnight,
Changed into an iron fruit heady with poisons, like night-
Shade. How did I not lose myself? Down three-star
Back ways, over floodlit bridges, guided by those stars
That steered toward now, hours later—as long as last night—
I woke the sleeping doorman with a yawn. Then, the matter
Of facing her. But—she hadn't noticed. There was the matter

Too of luggage to count, plane to catch, the papal diplomat her
Mother knew. . . . One apple-green case waits to be reunited
With the rest. The luna moth. I let her go. A matter
Of endangered species. Sunstruck, wobbly, a smattering
Of inflected throbs, she started underground. Nothing
I could urge made her fly up, fly home. What matter
Where I fly, she seemed to say, beating against the matted
Cloverleaf. There was no point but to watch as the day's
Earliest cock robin caught on, instinct's idée
Fixe. Worried by the wingspan and so the madder
For it, he made his dive for her. Head to head, the star-
Crossed pair shuddered in violent agreement. Now there stares

Back at me from a wet paving stone the envoy of someday
In my past, half a wing and its teardrop tail, nothing
So much as a scrap with its scribbled message *"Tonight."*
I'm reminded to look back, back through whatever the matter
Was, and see what's left over. It might as well be stars.

III

First Steps

1. 1946, 1957

How to put this exactly? I mean without
Hurting those who've known me long enough—
From long before the start, let's say—

To think what's called "hurt" is confined
To episodes at hand and waved aside,
The sky darker, more like itself again,

After the tracer's hairsbreadth giveaway.
And at the same time, without forgetting
What was left in the dark, entrenched,

The cold sweat of others' knowing rubbed
Off like earliest memories. Theirs,
I'm told, are of my refusing to take a step,

Backing across a roomful of women (my father
Was away at war), then crawling, crabwise,
Toward, or against, the half-foot drop

Onto the porch where they'd wait, the women,
A Member of the Wedding downturned
On my mother's knee while she clapped.

That is their memory. Mine is from the next year.
My birth had given my father the "points" to send him
Over the top, demobilized from sea to the shining
Jersey shore, to the women in my grandmother's house,
And me, the firstborn at last. One ear gone deaf
In enemy fire, his head would have been cocked
For his new comrade-in-arms' syllabic babble.
He liked to carry me shoulder-high, my legs locked
Around his head, hands in his hair. The infant Judith
Might have been so portrayed, pilasters instead of pier,
Her gaze intent on the future. Simple-minded revenge,
Like betrayal, at the heart is calm as a broadsword.
And I was screaming. *That* is my memory. It was when
He walked into the surf, as into a tent at night,

His head dipping, pretending to spill me, laughing.
The bladebright breaker. The loosening grip.
It's then I remember screaming. Both of us knew,
Or thought later, it wasn't the water. Years later
He said "You *never* trusted me." That cannot have been
True, because it still is not, old general idea.
Your hold is playfully tight to this day. No,
It must have been the water after all, its sharp
Command and penitent sucking, the mocking foam.

This country's wars come in decades. One later,
After a summer in camp, flagpole to fireside,
I'd fallen for my counsellor. His name was Red.
He slept during naptime and could be watched—
The namesake stubble, the sweatband, the upstart
Nipple, a dream's drool on his chin. That he seemed
Not to care for me at all, lined up beside me
For letters, mine from my mother, his from a girl
(Her snapshot was taped to the shelf over his bunk),
Became the secret I'd whisper to myself. The first
I'd kept. Or not that, but lying on a log, under
The cabin as under a shelf. The lake shone,
Then glittered with frog-spit.
                                      I kept that too
From Father Ayd during open-air confessional,
And learned to live in sin, though not in embarrassment.
What I kept to myself was one thing. What others
Could see for themselves, another. Sheepishly
I'd take communion. But I stuck it to the roof
Of my mouth, like a stamp from the Vatican, then wet
And unpeeled it into a shell I kept in my footlocker.
It was a time-bomb. My grandfather, who had died
In the arms of a memory of himself, a captain
At the Meuse, had replaced the detonator with a clock.
I kept it hidden, wound, ticking against the time
I was forgiven—what? The fight against the self?

August was home again. The sins told over and over
In the dark, I wrote them down, transfigured
Into a self-knowing tone, letter-perfect, to Red—
Then in lines of his own as a freshman at UVA.
They told tales on the camp cook, made up new endings
To stories he'd read at bedtime, and told my own,
Of "boring people" on the beach, of the impetigo
Scare, the drowned lifeguard. I never mentioned
My parents, that I had any, anyone else but whom
I'd cast out for his amusement, embarrassed by them,
As by this thin wafer, this thick wave, between us.
I'd given up hope to his long silence when one day
Two letters arrived for me. His "Hi, kid!" was one,
Under three Greek letters. "Gee, it was great
To hear from you, and all those funny stories.
Well, back to the grind." Lines, I thought, loaded
With feeling, to be read between tomorrow, not now.
The other was from the Ukrainian cook, more of the same
Warm misspelled gush she'd served up at camp.
My parents had "sampled" that on Parents Weekend,
So it was read aloud, to sniggers at precociousness.

And Red's? Red's was casually rushed to the beach
And buried, on a line with the pier and lifeguard shack,
So I could overturn the hourglass sand anytime
I cared. A day passed to show I didn't.
Pleasure postponed is redoubled in eternity,
The nuns had taught. Each imaginary grain—
Running, prickling, that much further, now
Closer—was. Each sentence, committed to memory,
Given a new gesture of gratitude at being dug out.
If sleep came, it came like three fraternity brothers
To say I'd been chosen too. Red. Hazing. It was dawn
When I woke. The tides had changed guard.

Love is up and about on tiptoe, the back steps,
Boardwalk, beach. Shells, empty-hearted homes,
Had washed up on maps of seaweed. I made for my X.

I look back on myself, as from my father's window,
Digging through a panic. How could I not
Have put it exactly? Each square circled twice,

Who'd put his trust in secrets kneeling there,
Fistfuls of sand thrown away on nothing,
Myself thrown down, away on the water.

2. 1871

Chasing on the margins of pond-waters, the sun
Then dips the sweet flag's quill into his mouth.
Glume and gloss, concentric drawls of whitebeard
Unspool around the stalk, its lazy hours widening
On a leaf, now shoreward drawn, and drawn up
By the boy there, the new contract, this America.

"Intense and loving comradeship, the personal
And passionate attachment of man to man—
Which, hard to define, underlies the lessons
And ideals of the profound saviors of every land
And age, which promises, when recognized
In manners and literature, the most substantial
Hope and safety of the future of these States. . . ."
America, then, as the place for this idea,
Closest because last discovered to the original,
The slip of fate. If we are angels unable
To fall, who move among tragedies unmoved,
We are Nature's first democracy. That estate
Precludes the claims of property, the thicket
Brambled with caprice, prick of father's blood-right,
Family's subsoil of exclusion, the accomplishing
Tribe, its branches and departments of hollowness
At heart, the organization of desire
And its hoopsnake political mythologies.
What have Americans to do with these?
Fitly born and bred apart to make
Their acquaintance with sky, air, water,
The quibble of dew on history's low relief.
Original relations. That is the democracy,
Sublimity in repose, slow cloud, hard clay.

The eye's devotions, the pond face to face
With the cloud's wet cargo in the hold
Of spirit, open to itself and to what passes
On it, unfinished as our idea has been.
So the eye of each man is on himself,
As once on the vast inland sea un-islanded

By others. The first desire is this silent
Communing. If we blink, or put off
A quiet providence, the cloud becomes a pillar,
A quaver, the mill and helpmeet, the law
Of the land. Conventions are what we make
Of them, the brood and license of example.
The past is a parent's myth, that pyramid
Built on capital, monopoly, and fear
To the ruling point that stares from a dollar,
The hungry child's eye. Myth sets
Rivals on, its dominion over time by division
Of space, men and women driven by death
Toward crisis or idolatry. Now the future
Is unloosed from that stage, those masks,
From the usual pleasures of those who do not
Believe in men. Income of its own accord,
Authority in itself, our democracy
Entrusts us to you, and him, and her,
Each ready to hand. And what is our care?
The breath gone into us. The air's caress.
Democracy is a sexual system, a secret
Society, the underground in each self,
All outcroppage cut back to eye and root
That stay, equal with the earth, to start
Again the idea of ourselves in this place.

Let us say the idea is where it belongs.
If still tentative, then gripped by purpose.
If humiliated, then buried deep in a ground
That does not sicken, in the sour peat-damp.
Let us say it is the wound under a compress,
A bullet-hole torn through the lung.
In the division hospital, a rank of young braves,
Mutilated boys, and our shy animal, a farmer's
Son, his frame naked, a coolness alert
In his limbs. By the pallet, a man takes down

A letter home, holds his hand, tousles his hair,
Sings the homemade music of friends passing over.
Flesh made word, the great poem of death is being
Written, underlying life, leaping time
That had wrecked them both together. O metaphysics!
What proves the democracy but soul and solitude?
The mind builds them to itself, then imagines
A nation of orbs in the free paths of heaven.
That touches a man closest. He will not let go
The boy's hand, even to put it at rest.

From the cat-eyed upper story windows
The Capitol's dome seemed to brood on
An old baffled romance. He's turned back in.
Somewhere the sun makes a western settlement,
Heat-thunder giving stamp to the prairie,
To the bronzed pond tilting toward the boy,
Armor out of the old books, advancing,
To a score of straw-colored psyches circling
Some everlasting there. A horse blanket up
Around his knees, and the lamplight speculating
In its own oil, he's bent to the last leaf.
"I can conceive such a community. . . ."

3. 1971

"What do *you* think?" The question my head
Had hit against for weeks. Where, I wanted
To know, was it at? The Health Service's
Ten Free Sessions, as if help were a home-trial
Vacuum, was the first question—along with Will,
The interne I was assigned to, a turtlenecked
California blond, young enough—a kid!—to trust
And condescend to at once. Rehearsed, reticent,
Those first fifty-minute hours soon gave way
To long distance calls that seemed to reach
An answering machine, its taped instructions
Androgynous, parental, the buzz both static
And signal for a message to be left.
                                        What?
"What do *you* think they want?" But wasn't
The point what I wanted? Wanted to say?
The welling point, shipwrecked on the verge
Of eyes fixed on Will, was made in sputtered
Remorse code: DON'T LET ME . . . DON'T LET ME GO.
That did the trick. That was what I'd wanted,
To be thought a special case, better than Lowell
A real life study, feelings not just historical
But intractably unnatural. (I was in the slough
Of a dissertation on the confessional poets
Whose hearts, those instruments of experience,
Were made blunt in verse. Or at my typewriter.)
Will agreed. Supervisors were consulted, action
Recommended, the visits extended. A pipe
Appeared. This would "take some work."
It did. I found his car in the lot, his address
In the hospital directory, glared at the backseat
Baby-bucket, and parked outside his complex.
Years before, I'd persuaded my parents to build
A swimming pool so I could change with my desires.
I was used to waiting, breath held off the deep
End, the uplit bodies diving over me. Will
Came home later, paler, his wife once flapped
Out a sheet, my car stalled. The sessions, too.

Getting the story out was hard, but at last
He opened up. His father the crossroads tyrant,
His younger brother the actor (later to play
Luke Skywalker), the time a new baby takes . . .
I drew out each grief, each grievance,
The understudy disaffection a patient ear
Makes the leading man. I hated myself
For doing it, fascinated by the curl another's
Story, like pipe smoke, takes around currents
Of sympathy, how anyone's secrets open the window
An inch. Had he ever . . . ? He *had*? Oh yes,
California. Do you want . . . ? We made a date.
He'd phone next week. The transference was complete.

By which I mean—the call soon came—I was
Transferred to another doctor, a greybeard
I couldn't afford. I called my father to cover
The fees, on trust, breezing through the reason.
(A year later, coming out to a pre-echo of "we know,"
I was told this doctor had telephoned, to cover
His fee, and told why. That silent wave my father
Had carried himself through—how long? Dear man.)
We sat for our face-off, the reason less clearly
Discernible beneath the shade of diplomas over him.
His nickname was mine, his surname what I wanted
To be—*Schreiber*. That desire up front, we plunged
Back, back to . . . a happy childhood.
How I hate to disappoint, and zero in on anything
To accuse. The time I screamed at my grandmother
Not to watch me change. The turd in the linen
Closet—will that do? An account of Red—yes?
No. Silence is a chapfallen look, a writer's
Imperative. The more I tried to please, the more
I grew convinced it wasn't a choice—like pleasing—
But a discovery. And his, not mine who'd always
Known what I wanted, and wondered now at earlier
Choices. They all seemed right, if unforeseen.
At prep school, the Jesuits had offered one:
Science or Classics, as if a syllabus for life.
At sixteen, there was no hesitating between

The knife and the verbwheel, its tombola spin
Of voices, declensions, conjugations, exceptions
To the rule of its own momentum. Through its little
Thumbed cardboard window I could see the future
I imagined was an iron cot behind a Chinese screen,
An Oxford text propped on the scraped oak table.
There was everything to recommend it but a body.
I was told to recite Homer aloud, between spoonfuls
Of applesauce, in the basement—what was that
Meant to hide? Not a taste of sealife, but the fact
That metaphor enlivens loneliness. The body is literal.
Wasn't that what Achilles came to know, came to grief
Upon? I slumped in my chair.

                            And on my barstool perch
Of eager nonchalance, boredom paired with bashfulness,
To pick out, those nights, beneath the revolving disco
Balls of facets, trick spots and flanks of stop-and-go,
A possible evening star who'd highlight by daybreak,
So help me, an end to fast and loose routines
Stunningly echoed underfoot by the thud—or therapy—
Of mindless concentration, the contact high of someone
Else's Rush, the umpteenth blast of jungle drums
Or "Smarty Pants," the sinking feeling of having been
Here—was it called Plato's or Circe's Cave?—too often.
The floor was full of them, bodies, the cavaliers
In designer jeans, busy at their job of being new
By flaunting it, stuffed into the glamor of types,
Dropout honcho, wasted dopehead, a guardsman
With advanced degrees, each partnered by the trance
He'd turned himself on to. Into that corral (*Whistle*
Siren   Wail) a black magic voice is luring
So much beef on the hoof, their flickering, slow-motion
Flail of dream-sex, fist and heel, heads thrown back
To the promise of more. ". . . What you've been waiting for."

More what? What did I think? The waiting
Seemed interminable. All that small talk
While a fantasy hurriedly undressed was getting
Nowhere. I told him so. He wasn't choosy.

"Rejection especially tells us what we want,
Now doesn't it?" What I wanted was a body,
My body, not the versions of it here or there,
Neither the fear, as if under water too long,
The last breath wrung bubbled to break
On the arching image, nor the trembling
Under a sheet, but a body that feels itself
In the world of men, a weight that bears.
My draft on Lowell was done. The bar as well
Had been raided. Heart racing, I walked out
Of the office into a sudden heat. The news
Was being delivered up and down the street.

4.

The spirit sets about its task, but slowly,
Preoccupied with theories of itself:
Escaping trace element, the doll-mother
Propped on the god's knee, the careworn case
All the samples are in. Take this first one.

A baptismal dress, laid out now on the couch,
Its bobbined, spreading family tree of lace,
The stains of storage and ceremony the same
Color as the weak tea served after I,
My father and grandfather before me too,
Had worn it. What of that first water
Of belief? A golden-rule chrism is poured
On it, and candles lit to make such
A light no evil can see its way into.
"Infantile sexual researches," could
They begin there, once the senses are cured
In soul? The pediatrician had warned
My mother, the analyst later reminded me,
Of what are called hydraulic pressures,
The up-and-down of desires satisfied
At the cost of long-drawn-out helplessness—
As if there were some amniotic preference
To hug the shore than chance the open sea,
To watch the waves undone to a ruffle of froth
Around my feet. My feet. . . . I was past three
Before I learned to walk. Dandled and fed,
I sat in her lap, the performing self
Who, as they say, had a vocabulary—
Petal and oar, bubble and wand, each
Dipped into the font of her approval,
Each come at last to be submerged in what
It was, my belief, my whole erotic life.

Like a letter pushed under the future's
Door, that dress can be packed back up
In the case. Pull out this Venetian mask,
A character called Sintomo, and assume

Beneath the marbled-paper complexion
His phalloid nose, his leering eye-slits.
A disguise both mocks and abets whatever
Power wants to pretend is right. The mercurial
Thief steals not to have but to be
Something, his stolen goods a fantasy
Acted out, consumed, controlled by
A self in love with its own images
Bent to the glass where he makes
Himself up, prodigal of conscience,
Outsider "I" of the poem. I ought to know.

And here, shabby as a carpet slipper, is
My old dog-eared Selected Auden. St. Wiz!
Subdued to what you worked in, the foiled
Caresses from which thought is born.
Look to its motive, you taught, and not
The choice love makes. The bald giant
On the runway, whose name is always Need,
Picks at random, his makeshift eye,
His mouth that gives the lie to another
Tongue, his homespun heart worn to rags
On someone else's body—anybody's.
Love builds its house on sand, on ordinary
Swoons and unworthy objects as gladly
As on the motherland with its ricks and sheds,
Or the gilded idolized imaginings
We wander through. Love is analogy,
What suits. How cannily you moralized
The body, insisted guilt lie down with lust,
Wooed the superior mind with dirty secrets,
And made your prayer that love be not
Perfection but the energy attracting us
Toward it, any longing that fits a god.

And between the pages, pressed to that wound
He'd sent his letter to, a wildflower
Itself now paper-thin, a splayed sun-bow—
Covenant with what memory it was meant

To recall? The boy I was? Or the figure
Of the youth I am in this poem? The future
Sometimes seems former lives, or stages
Of a life, drawing them out of the past,
The flashing moment's hasp snapped up.
The future that boy desired and feared
Depends on our converging, expansive
Recognition of something more than either
The boy or his guardian could in no time
Want to make of it, a past less deviant
Than defiant, struggling to be in touch
With spirit. The lover is an older man
On purpose, inspirer in this pastoral
Of hero-worship, and love's the yearning
Text, best beloved and still puzzled over.
The years come up, the sun goes down
Tonight as if into the case itself
Whose cover is fastened now, and once again
I'll turn to walk downstairs, back
Into the empty house, into the waiting arms.

IV

Mineralogy Object

JM's

Not a cockatoo or wiffle ball, no demitint
Sylphide on a bee-studded sheer of midnight,
Her wings, if torn away, in a drawer beneath.
No cork worlds tossing on a sea of space
Charted by last century imperialist longings
For heroes in the arms of the Old Style.

Now is a stereopticon of sorts,
Of *Variétés de Minéralogie*.
Each footlight letter on this keyboard's
Shadow box squints knowingly on
A smoked glass proscenium, front and center
An enlightenment soon lost in thought.

So *this* is the mind's eye. This compulsion
To repeat, in diminishing stages, whatever
Script is drawn from the same few favorites.
(Pages into one, Echo pines on the shore,
Wavering disregard in every wave
Farewell, the fable become psychology.)

In our small case, it is a photograph,
The studio props—divan's plush and matching
Foreshortened civic vista—predictably frayed,
Its subject all too easily seen through.
An empty figure, in fact, for the fictions
That follow, mock-ups either one of us

Used to linger over the more for taking them
As less than real. No, not memories:
They are exact and rendered by the moment's
Timely paragraph. Matters, then, of the heart
Whose traces, at a later touch, explode
Into a troupe of stars. Here are four:

1. Verdâtre

The glazed swell
    of spring,
pitted with flaws,
    ice-weals
an oxide wash blurs
    into slippery
remarks overheard
    by dazed
half-dead tulips,
    the dozen
you brought, those
    damp curls—
it's here! Their lips
    curl too,
the pout of what can
    die, a passage
of flowers, dreambare.
    "A great strain
to finish the work."
    The genital knot
of second green themes
    from whose cramped
beginnings there rises,
    plucked,
these remaining ideas.
    One sticks
out, a febrile pirate
    stem lifting
the girl high, higher
    than her gasp,
than any withheld kiss
    the nerves allay.
A wordless chorus
    spills over
their song. They turn
    on that song.

2. Rougeâtre

Under the blackboard's bell curve eclipse
A rule was drawn that took: Opposites Attract.

Having just ended up in *The Red and The Black*
She knew attraction's opposite too—hearts

With one purpose, the paper ghosts that start
A cleric's summer romance from molten types

To historical foolscap, blotted flare-script.
Her right eye stays open behind that cutout,

Trained on his skywriting, the closemouthed
Track it takes, first noon and now its familiar

Night, that changing bag. The painkillers'
Chalky taste leaves a bubble on her lips.

Hindsight fades, so needle wits assume.
"What will those sweet bywords not presume?"

3. Noirâtre

    The beat, a feathery panic, tapped out
    Night after night. Who's been calling?

Old wire recorders pick her up now.
    She's launched the slotted raft,
    A chicken-head zodiac still reeling
With the houngan's rum. It slowly sinks in.

Rapturous clay beads float down the spine,
    Stop from house to house—
    Each one an angel, the maman says.
I believe her, this time. Her mask, clenched

And jutting, is of A Young King in Love.
    He knows. She freezes a moment
    Too long, a half-heard voice grumbles.
—"He's not himself. Too heavy. All spleen.

    Remember when he was young, made up
    Like a star, worked by coin and plunger?"

4. Cléopâtre

Tangled in sheet
Lightning an hour to dawn,
She's wakened by her dream, a cry
The wheeling gods processed behind.
His spectral armor's on,
The powers agreed,
One bright tear shooting down.

A parsec shorter
Her face, and then the world's,
Would change. Vanity is prince
Of her revenge, his baldequins
Taut with black-pearled
Contempt for her
One bright tear shooting down.

What is it like
To live in the sky? To moon
Over the dark, cloud-mounted point
To pole? To yield, and then enjoin?
The missing hours are her room,
That room inside
One bright tear shooting down.

But now switch
The light, put on her crown,
As if this filament's lash were all
The Milky Way, or a compass called
My cameo. For ends her own
Her will's my wish:
One bright tear shooting down.

Above Beirut

The worrier's twisting, and leans to kiss the words.
What's not yet pledged may one day spill in chords,

Their round of shells, but none—*not one word*—is apt
To land just here, inside my mud-and-tile riverbed.

It is harmony not anger that seeks to divide,
A diacritical moon over the scroll of tides

Out the lone oud's open mouth. Alexander's lobe
Hangs so, down from the mosque's bellowing dome,

And atomic clouds, fastened as Buddha's halo.
Breaking the surface calm—to wipe the squalor

Of slow dying from her face—of a cloud-rutted trough
In her settlement, a refugee crouches in the Shuf.

Murderous for change, from the sandbag pillow
New reasons rush by, impossible to love or ignore,

Each day closer, on the breast, across the eye,
The urgent hand brushed off to prolong the desire

For it. Now the other side lobs a dawn by halves—
The automatic fire, and stupid speaking of ourselves.

Montale: Motets

III

Rime at the panes; the patients
always enclosed, always at loose
ends; and over the tables
endless readings of the cards.

Your exile, say. Again I think
over mine, and of the morning
when I heard between the cliffs
that ballerina bomb shuffling.

The nightly game, the fireworks,
took forever: as if a holiday.

Then a rough wing grazed my hand,
but to no end: this is not your card.

XVI

The flower that rehearses
at the edge of the gorge
its forget-me-not
has no strain more joyous, more clear
than what emptiness we bridge.

A rasp of iron comes between us,
the pig-headed azure won't return.
In a palpable heat the funicular drops me
at the opposite station, already dark.

After de Kooning

If there were a letter to mail
Beginning "Most beautiful Bathsheba—
Because . . ." she would not stop

Until you'd got it, the lightning
Streak a finger plucks, the breasts
Of rainstorm still potato fields away,

And teeth a vane turned into the wind,
Eyes of a child behind the railcar window.
The weather keeps her in, writing.

"I've led such a sad life since.
Whole days without eating,
Nights without sleeping. You would

See me instead of this, if presence
Were a power to console. But I have
The liberty of staying here, the little

Wooden cage outside the old Parliament.
The protest continues . . ." It does.
I saw it. European security

In the balance. And her husband's
36th birthday. How celebrated
In the asylum? Perhaps they draw

A map. Possible places. Horizon.
Swamp. Jewish cemetery. Acknowledgment
Lifelike in its ability to gut with fire.

Lifelong, the scream into the teeth of it.
Who travels through this world to make it
Plain is the shadow in the white of her eyes.

Ovid's Farewell

What was my fault? A book, and something I saw.
　　The one he never read, the other
　　　　He was author of.
　　Not his daughter—her adulteries
　　Were with boys from other men's beds, mine
Merely with women from other men's poems—

But his empire. He had long since made his Peace
　　And thereby the fear that would keep it,
　　　　The commerce of praise
　　And the short sword, a vomit that cleanses
　　The palate. The same horses that tear
The flesh at night by day drive over the tribes.

The quarry falls into his toils. We all have
　　Our methods of conquest. Even me.
　　　　Mine was the dove-drawn
　　Chariot named Illusion, cockeyed
　　Laurel crown, and whispers on the way.
I could have chosen another theme—the sons

Who kill their fathers, the brothers who salt each
　　Other's cities, or the empire's spawn,
　　　　Glistered avenues
　　To sacrifice, bloody baths and nets.
　　But mine was love-in-idleness scratched
On an apple. In that sweet anatomy

Of desire he smells a treason. Woodland
　　Shrines and pillow-books, the subversive
　　　　Mirror, its fragrant
　　Incestuous tear beneath the bark—
　　These conspire against the down-turned
Thumb, policy for sale with chalk on its feet

And locks around its heels. When gods make themselves
　　Into men, they become less than men,
　　　　A human desire.

When men would be gods, they pass new laws
And strengthen the Family. Like gods,
Then, they breed contempt and their own betrayal.

Though whatever work I tried turned under me
Into verse, the spells and bullroarers
Of family life
Resisted all but a low satire,
The cold late supper of everyday.
I had chosen and loved a life in the shade,

A cough, certain oils, her blue lips from under.
It was from such shadows that I saw
His daughter come to
Kick against his rule. I ignored her,
Of course, but one of her slaves had seen
Me, and seen a way to pay for his freedom.

Slaves, our living shades, are like readers, always
Eager for a new master. Lovers
Look for somewhere else
To live, and when they find it, they ask
The poet for passage. Now it is
My turn to pay for love. First my poems made me

Friends, now fame has made my enemies. Tomis?
In Greek the word means "amputation"
And so he would have
My tongue cut out. The title is his,
Not mine, called the Master of Changes.
The life to come will be all the past, the world

Before Rome, rough skins and grunts and frenzied wasps
In their rain-ruined tents. I hear they
Have only one god
To worship. How can one god fill up
The sky? Or answer for this wrangle
In the heart? Perhaps the sky there in Tomis—

Where the Kid is drowned under waves, and the Bear
        Kept chained to his pole—is small enough.
                I am to be changed
        Into a *character*—a woman
        Whose lover is at wine and gaming
With knuckle-bones. She smears her eyes with charcoal

So he will not see her—if he should look up—
        Looking away. Or, if not that girl,
                Then what is the same,
        A ghost, skirling inside an urn called
        Tomis. Flattery! That is the work
Of a woman and a ghost. Let us play them

Tonight, before I am both, and you neither.
        My friends tell me, Fabia, I am
                Married to story,
        And so to change. But men do not change,
        They grow old, and grow afraid. I have
Left wives before, but not one I loved. There, there,

. . . The very poem of Troy is enacted!
        The fires wept on, the hearth gods smashed,
                The old queen's ashes
        Passed from hand to hair. They are afraid
        For themselves, my friends, and come to offer
Advice like gentlemen. I may as well count

On the critics. Not that I mind to beg them
        For it. Their pity is a fool's gold
                And dealt in Caesar-
        Struck coin. One will pay my ferry-ride.
        But what shall I take from this last night?
A book? A strong leather cloak? A pen to blind

Myself with petitions? We all live someone
        Else's story, so we may know how
                It turns out. I have

Taken something before, then . . . But what?
My brother's life. Yes. No one knows that,
Nor ever thought it then, thirty years ago.

One day, in an island of wheatspikes,
We were playing our war, his mattock
Up in the noonlight's
Angry hour, my barrel-siding
Like an elephant on the mountain.
Having leaped into some last ditch of defense,

His angular stillness was itself both call
And surrender. Not meant to win,
I wondered, then saw
The snake, black standard of an army
Marching off under the world. I watched
Its tongue question the distance to the boy.

When it stopped, the tale came to my lips. "Brother,
Show respect to the god, a sea-borne
God, come to favor—"
My own panic made up its mission—
"The purple shells on his cave's ceiling
Were tongues that told of the Sun's only daughter

Who kept his light from the dead, their souls the chaff
Winnowed from life. If a snake could slip
Into the mill's pin. . . ."
Calmed, I continued, and backed away.
He turned to me, as one who believes
Will turn the page, and as he turned, the snake struck.

The stone in my throat was that one said
To turn black in the hand of a liar.
Dog's milk was rubbed on
His gums, a wolf's liver in thin wine
Was forced, and cow dung through a fresh reed.
Superstitions save what's no longer wanted.

He died. He died as silent as I've remained.
    The next day I dreamed the god came back,
        Had truly returned
    And come to the chamber of the dead.
    My brother, pale as a grain fallen
On a cloth, recognized him and stood, head bowed,

Intent on his part. Then the god took him up
    To Hercules whose quiver behind
        Is a crown of stars.
    But the great Serpent coiled in night,
    As the boy approached, wound itself round
The hero's outstretched arm who was to hold

Him fast by his side, a friend to his labors.
    So the boy in error was taken
        Further up, farther
    Away, too far to be seen by men.
    But I have, there between the bowstring
And the shaft, whenever I look up for a line.

Exile—a boy into death, the bit of life
    Stranded in a song, or its singer—
        Is the end of our
    Belief. It comes to pass, the last change
    As the first, from a stream of star-shot
Wonderment that falls down to our home on earth.

Notes

THE PALACE DWARF: The Ducal Palace, Mantua.

MINERALOGY OBJECT: Construction by Joseph Cornell, 1939.

AFTER DE KOONING: It happened that the same day I saw the de Kooning retrospective at the Whitney Museum and was again struck by the power of his series of "Women" from the early 1950's, there appeared in the *New York Times* an article about Avital Shcharansky's continuing protest on behalf of her husband, Anatoly, the Soviet dissident held in Christopol prison.

OVID'S FAREWELL: Ovid himself, in the single mysterious reference he made to the cause of his exile from Rome, spoke of *"carmen et error"*—his poem (the slyly erotic *Ars Amatoria*) and a mistake. It used to be thought that by the latter was meant he had witnessed some sexual "indiscretion" committed by Augustus's promiscuous daughter Julia—whose behavior finally led the emperor to act on his stern laws against adultery and have her banished as well. But I prefer the argument by recent historians that what Ovid had actually witnessed was a political conspiracy against the emperor of which Julia was a (perhaps unwitting) part.

Among the facts about Ovid's life we do know for certain are that he had an older brother who died suddenly when still relatively young, and that his third and beloved wife was named Fabia. It is to her that this poem is purportedly addressed, on the night before he is to leave for the bleak, freezing penal settlement at Tomis, on the Black Sea near the mouth of the Danube, among the barbaric Getae.

The Kid (Capricorn) and the Bear (Ursa Major), Hercules and the Serpent, are all four of them constellations.